SCIENCE ENCYCLOPEDIA

LIGHT, MACHINES AND PARTICLE PHYSICS

Om KIDZ

An imprint of Om Books International

Contents

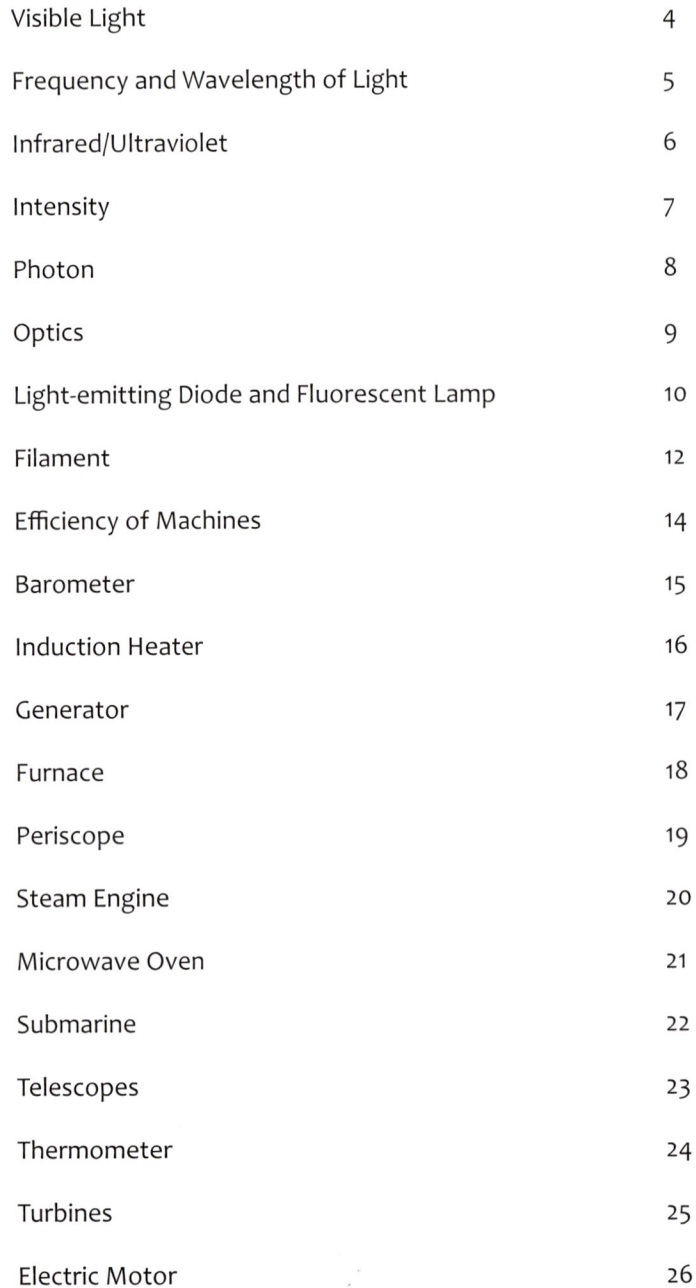

Visible Light	4
Frequency and Wavelength of Light	5
Infrared/Ultraviolet	6
Intensity	7
Photon	8
Optics	9
Light-emitting Diode and Fluorescent Lamp	10
Filament	12
Efficiency of Machines	14
Barometer	15
Induction Heater	16
Generator	17
Furnace	18
Periscope	19
Steam Engine	20
Microwave Oven	21
Submarine	22
Telescopes	23
Thermometer	24
Turbines	25
Electric Motor	26
Splitting an Atom	28
Fatal Fusion	29
Nuclear Power	30
Quantum Physics	32

LIGHT AND ITS SOURCES

When it comes to the scientific and logical explanation of concepts such as light and its basics, it is stated as nature's way of moving energy from point A to point B. Light is referred to as a form of energy that is produced from a specific source. Millions of fast travelling photons make up this light and are responsible for the speed of the overall light wave. But how does light travel? The answer is simple. It travels in the form of a wave. In fact, light is defined as a travelling wave not unlike a string. Every light wave travels at approximately 300,000 km per second and can go through vacuum as well; for example, when it travels through space. However, when travelling through denser materials, be it from the atmosphere of a planet to a simple piece of glass, the speed of a light wave slows down considerably. Let's find out why this happens.

SCIENCE ENCYCLOPEDIA

Visible Light

An electromagnetic spectrum is the combination of a range of different colours of lights. Visible light, that is, visible spectrum is that portion of the electromagnetic spectrum, which can be detected by the human eye. An average human eye often responds to 390–700 nanometre (nm) wavelengths of light and this is known as the visible spectrum.

The invention

In the seventeenth century, English physicist Isaac Newton first named this principle "spectrum", which is Latin for appearance, after his discovery of the concept of a prism's capacity to disassemble and reassemble white light. There are, sometimes, unsaturated colours like pink, purple or even magenta, which the human eyes and brain might not be capable of distinguishing. All those colours that contain only one wavelength are usually known as spectral colours or pure colours.

Dispersal of white light into various colours by a diamond.

Spectrum

A spectrum of pure colours is continuous as it has no clear boundaries between one colour and the next. Visible wavelength can pass through a region of the electromagnetic spectrum, the optical window, which allows it to pass largely undisturbed through Earth's atmosphere itself. Many species can see light frequencies that are beyond a human's visible spectrum. A white light, which is visible to us, is composed of seven colours of different frequencies. They are violet, indigo, blue, green, yellow, orange and red. In short, VIBGYOR. By remembering the word "VIBGYOR" (consists of the first letter of the seven constituent colours of white colour) one can remember these seven colours. These colours are often visible in nature. For example, the rainbow that is formed in the sky when we get sunshine during or immediately after the rains. This happens because sunshine is broken up into seven colours by water droplets in the atmosphere. The curvature of the rainbow is due to the different wavelengths of different colours.

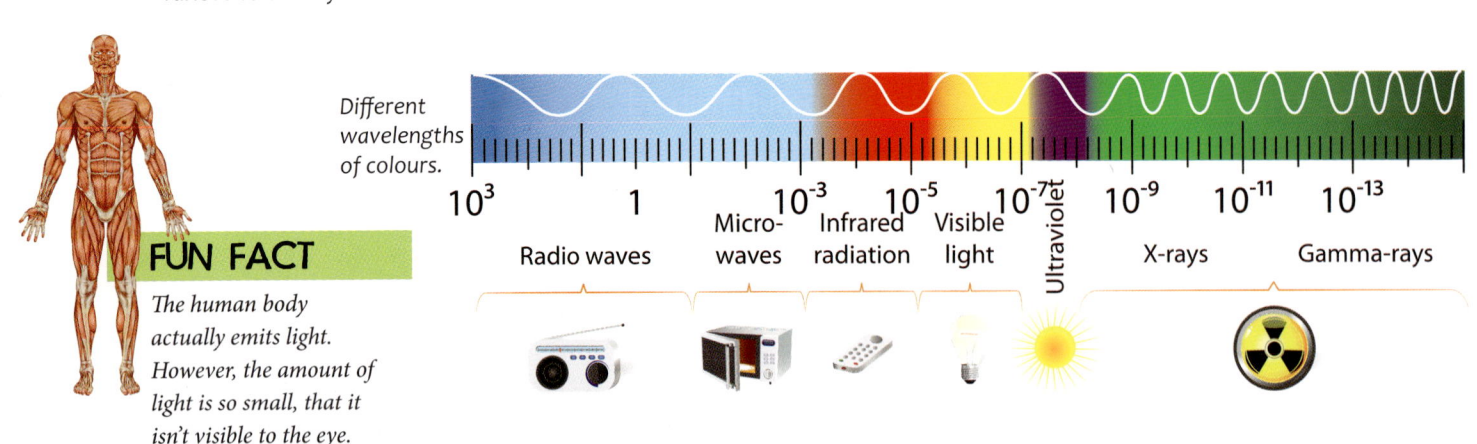

Different wavelengths of colours.

10^3 — Radio waves
1
10^{-3} — Microwaves
10^{-5} — Infrared radiation
10^{-7} — Visible light
Ultraviolet
10^{-9} — X-rays
10^{-11}
10^{-13} — Gamma-rays

FUN FACT
The human body actually emits light. However, the amount of light is so small, that it isn't visible to the eye.

LIGHT, MACHINES AND PARTICLE PHYSICS

Frequency and Wavelength of Light

In terminologies used for light, the quantity that is known to be "waving" in the electromagnetic field can be described with a particular wavelength and wave diagram. The Greek alphabet "lambda" is normally used to notify the wavelength of light. There are many such units of length used for depicting the wavelength of electromagnetic radiation.

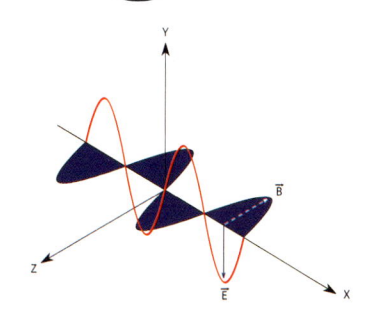

Wavelength of light

If we were to measure light on a scale, it would quite literally be like a wave. Consider a straight line. The wave would begin from the starting point of this line, moving upwards like a climbing graph, then downwards to intersect the straight line and continue below like a dipping graph. Eventually, the wave would again come up and intersect the straight line. The important thing to remember is, that the length the wave covers over the straight line is equal to the length that it covers under the straight line. Also, the distance between the two highest points is the same as the distance between the two lowest points. This distance is called a wavelength.

A rainbow.

Frequency of light

If we have to measure the frequency of light, we have to take another variable into consideration; time. In that case, we consider that the straight line that we spoke of earlier represents time. Now, the wave keeps rising and falling as described earlier. However, the number of times that the wave reaches a certain height in a given amount of time is called its frequency. In simpler terms, if we consider the number of times that a wave reached its highest point within 1 second, that is described as the frequency of the wave. Therefore, frequency is defined as the number of times a wave rises or falls within a given amount of time.

A prism dispersing colours of different wavelengths.

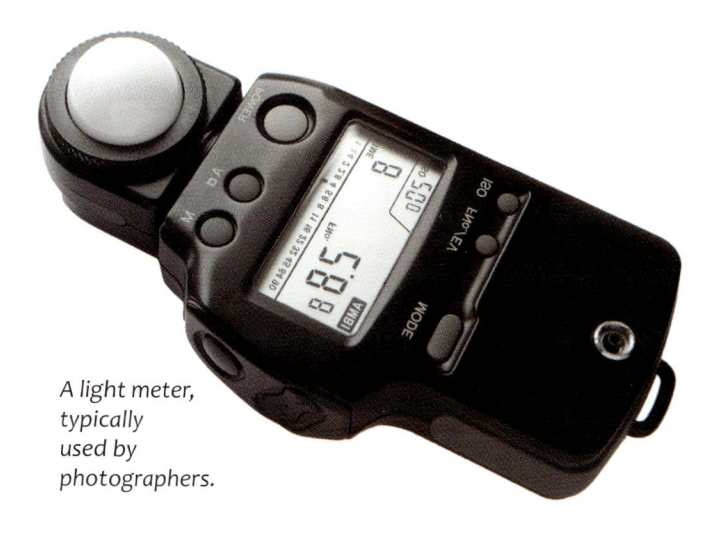

Measuring the spectrum

If we were to consider the spectral colours and measure their wavelength and frequency, we would see that red has the lowest wavelength and frequency. Hence, it falls on the lowest part of the spectrum and violet has the highest wavelength and frequency, putting it at the other end of the spectrum. They all lie in order of the "VIBGYOR".

A light meter, typically used by photographers.

SCIENCE ENCYCLOPEDIA

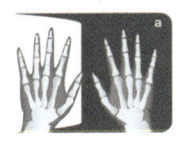

Infrared/ Ultraviolet

The invisible radiant energy of electromagnetic radiation which has longer wavelengths than visible light is known as infrared. On the other hand, the invisible radiant energy of electromagnetic radiation which has shorter wavelengths than visible light is known as ultraviolet rays.

Uses of infrared light

English astronomer Sir William Herschel discovered an invisible light with a wavelength less than that of red light in 1880. This light came to be known as infrared light. There are many uses of the infrared light. One of its major properties that has been put to use is its sensitivity to heat. Hence, this light has been used in making night vision goggles that enable one to see objects in the dark based on the object's heat signature. This technology has also been used to make infrared space telescope that enables the viewer to get a better view into space. Infrared thermal imaging cameras are used to detect the overheating of electrical apparatus, detect change of blood flow in the human body, etc.

Uses of ultraviolet light

Johann Wilhelm Ritter, a German physicist, discovered violet rays with a wavelength that was more than that of violet light. This light came to be known as ultraviolet light. Ultraviolet light is available abundantly in nature. The Sun is a major source of ultraviolet light, also known as UV light. In fact, our bodies need UV light to create Vitamin D. This light has a special property of causing chemicals to react and cause certain substances to glow. UV light is used in many ways. Since it increases the rate of melanin production in our skin, it is used in tanning beds to make the skin tan faster. Because it has the ability to make certain substances fluoresce, it is used in the detection of fingerprints, bodily fluids and blood traces at crime scenes amongst many other things.

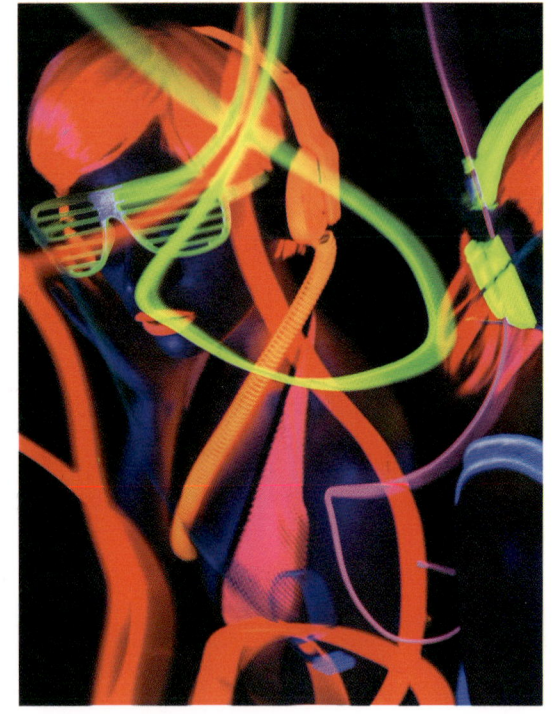

Neon colours glow under ultraviolet lights.

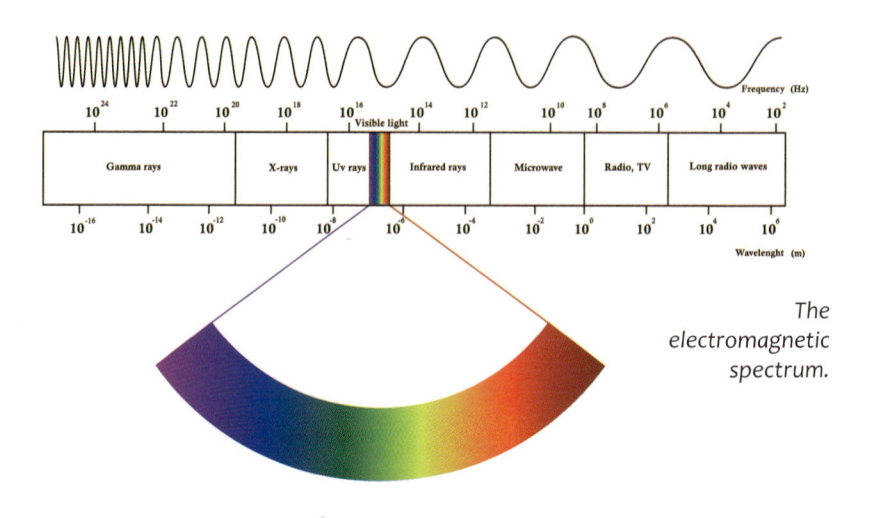

The electromagnetic spectrum.

LIGHT, MACHINES AND PARTICLE PHYSICS

Intensity

Many aspects of light are measured as its intensity. Everything from a light's radiance to its luminosity can be measured under the umbrella of intensity. In physics, the simple meaning of the term intensity is the energy that is transferred per unit area.

What is the intensity of light?

Usually, scientists don't mention light in terms of waves and amplitude, as light by itself doesn't change when it travels through water or air. Intensity is like the brightness measure of light and can be easily measured at a rate at which light energy can be delivered to a chosen or given unit of surface area.

A light meter.

Solar panels with photoreceptor cells.

FUN FACT

Fish are more aware of their predators when there is a greater intensity of light. This is why they're easier to catch at dawn or dusk rather than in the middle of the day.

Application of intensity of light

Knowing the intensity of light can come in handy in many ways. For example, the intensity of sunlight on a solar panel when multiplied by the area of the panel can specify how much power is available to use solar appliances at home. A lot of simplified equations and formulas can help an individual calculate the energy per unit time to run different solar appliances and thus save up on a lot of energy wastage as well. Similarly, when we purchase bulbs, we look at the watts that it consumes. This gives us an indication of the amount of brightness or the intensity of the bulb. We can assume that a bulb with higher watts usage will provide more intensity of light or will be able to brighten a larger area in the house.

Different ways of measuring the intensity of light

There are several electronic components that are light-sensitive and measure the intensity of light. Photoelements or solar cells generate electricity when light shines on them. They can be present in small battery chargers and small lamps. The advantage of these photocells is that the electrical current they deliver increases strictly with the light intensity. Photoresistors are small components whose electrical resistance reduces when light shines on them. They help increase the brightness of a display in areas where there is an increase in the surrounding light. Photoresistors are usually made to have the same spectral sensitivity as the human eye. Photodiodes and phototransistors are very small components that permit a greater electric current to pass through when light shines on them. They are used to sense the movement of a computer mouse.

SCIENCE ENCYCLOPEDIA

Photon

A photon is the basic unit of all electromagnetic radiation. It is a mass-less, charge-less, stable quantum of light. Photons exhibit the properties of both waves and particles. They are not made up of any smaller particles as they themselves are basic particles. Hence, they are also known as elementary particles.

What is a photon?

In 1900, German physicist Max Planck first suggested the existence of photons while he was working on black-body radiation. Planck proposed that the energy of electromagnetic waves is released as discrete "packets" of energy. Later, Albert Einstein suggested that electromagnetic waves can only exist as these packets of energy, which he called "light quantum".

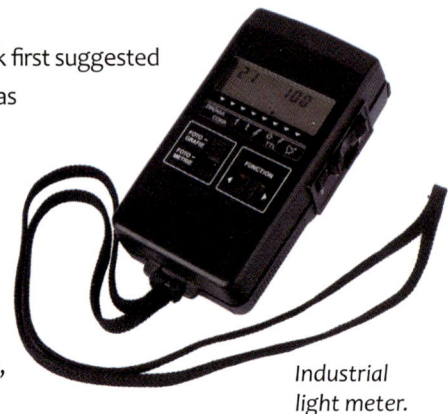

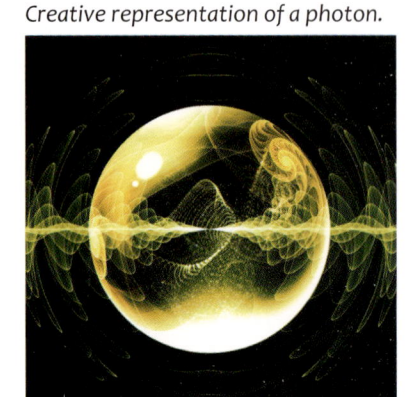

Industrial light meter.

Creative representation of a photon.

Photon properties

A photon can travel through empty space at a speed of almost 299,792 km/second. The ratio of the speed of photons in a particular medium to their speed in a vacuum is called velocity factor. It is always between 0 and 1, and depends on the wavelength to some extent. The shorter the wavelength of an electromagnetic disturbance, the more energy each photon contains. At any specific wavelength, every photon has the same amount of energy. The brilliance or intensity is a function of the number of photons striking a given surface area per unit time. Photons can be destroyed/created when radiation is absorbed or emitted.

Application of photon

Using this hypothesis, Einstein explained the photoelectric effect of electromagnetic radiation, which earned him the Nobel Prize in 1921. Einstein proved that photons are actually physical quanta of light as they show properties of both wave and particle. Accepting the dual nature of photons, it was possible to explain the photoelectric effect and other phenomena caused by electromagnetic radiation. Photons have numerous technological applications, particularly in experiments and devices that deal with the photoelectric effect.

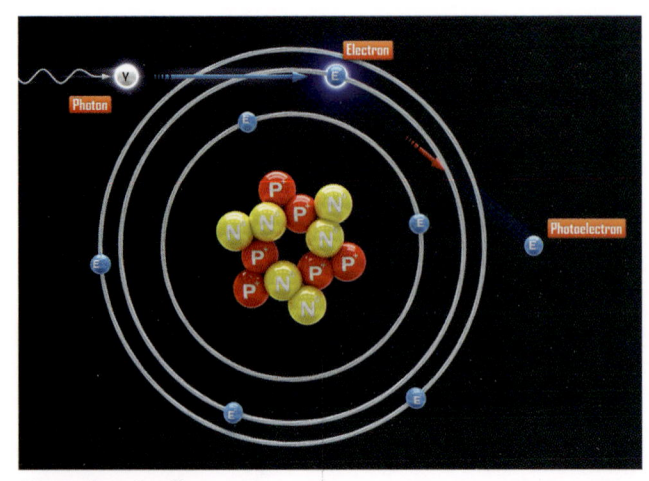

Photoelectric effect.

LIGHT, MACHINES AND PARTICLE PHYSICS

Optics

Optics is the branch of physics that deals with light, its properties and behaviour, and phenomena caused by or related to light. Light is an electromagnetic radiation; thus, optics also explains the generation, propagation, detection and other behaviour of electromagnetic waves like X-rays, microwaves and radio-waves. This branch of physics deals with three principal ranges of light – visible, ultraviolet and infrared light.

A camera works on the principles of optics.

What is optics?

Optics is the study of the science of light. It is an inextricable part of human life. The human eye contains photoreceptor rod cells and cone cells, which act as natural optical devices. The eye works on the basic principle of optics, which has various uses in the field of medicine, surgery and construction of optical devices like spectacles and corrective lenses. Optics is separated into two major areas: geometrical optics, which deals with how light moves and where it goes, and physical optics, which deals with the nature of light and the interaction between light and matter.

Applications of optics

Optical devices like magnifying glasses, photographic lenses, rear-view mirrors, microscopes and telescopes are all applications of optical phenomena and principles. Zoom camera with long focus is one of the modern applications of optics in the field of photography. Newer fields like opto-physics, optical-engineering and opto-electronics are coming up to encompass all phenomena and technologies involving light and other electromagnetic radiations.

Quantum optics

Most optical phenomena, like reflection, refraction and diffraction can be explained using classical electromagnetic views of light. However, some phenomena like photoelectric effect can be explained only by quantum optics that considers the wave–particle duality of light. Quantum optics have applications in the fields of physics and engineering along with practical uses. Lasers, photomultipliers, light-emitting diodes, photovoltaic cells, CCDs, etc., all function on the basic principles of quantum optics.

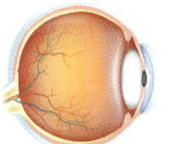

A microscope working on the basic principles of quantum optics.

SCIENCE ENCYCLOPEDIA

Light-emitting Diode and Fluorescent Lamp

Light-emitting diodes or LEDs are semiconductor devices that produce visible light when an electrical current passes through them. Light-emitting diodes are basically a solid state lighting (SSL), as are organic light-emitting diodes (OLEDs) and light-emitting polymers (LEPs). LED lighting differs from incandescent and compact fluorescent lighting in various ways. In order to work, an electrical current, "I", passes through the semiconductor material, which eventually illuminates the tiny-sized light sources known as LEDs.

LED colours

Many common LED colours are available today. In reality, there is no such thing as a "white" LED. To get a white light, the type we use for lighting residential as well as industrial premises, different coloured LEDs are mixed with a phosphor material that converts the colour of light. Colourful LEDs are frequently used in traffic signals, indicators, power buttons on computers/laptops, etc.

LED applications

LEDs are now being incorporated into bulbs and fixtures for general lighting uses. LEDs can be made in various sizes and can be designed in different shapes. Some LED bulb solutions may look like the usual light bulbs. Some LEDs light fixtures can have LEDs built in as a permanent light source. LEDs are directional light sources, which means they emit light in a specific direction, unlike the incandescent and the compact fluorescent bulbs, where emission of light and heat takes place in all directions.

Common incandescent lights.

FUN FACT

Once used, fluorescent bulbs shouldn't be thrown into the trash. The bulbs have small amounts of mercury in them. This classifies them as "hazardous waste".

LIGHT, MACHINES AND PARTICLE PHYSICS

Applications of LEDs

LEDs can be divided into four major categories. First, they can be used as visual signals where light travels more or less directly from the source to the human eye. This application can be used to convey a message or meaning. Second, it can illuminate objects to provide a visual response of those objects. Third, LEDs could be used to measure and interact with processes involving no human vision. Fourth, LEDs operate in narrow band light sensors in a reverse-bias mode and respond to incident light, instead of emitting light.

Fluorescent lamp

A fluorescent lamp or bulb is a low pressure mercury (Hg) vapour gas-discharge device, which uses fluorescence to yield visible light. When an electric current is passed through the gas, the mercury vapours get excited and produce short-wave UV light, which then causes the phosphor coating inside the bulb to glow brightly. A fluorescent bulb/lamp converts the electrical energy to light with higher efficiency as compared to incandescent bulbs/lamps. The life of a simple white LED is forecasted to be between 3500 and 5000 hours, which is much higher than its competitor's incandescent bulb that has a life of 750–2000 hours. The lifetime of a conventional bulb is determined by the longevity of its filament; however, the lifetime of LEDs is determined differently. The lifetime of LEDs is defined as the mean number of hours till the light falls to 70 per cent of the initial brightness, in the unit of Lumens.

Efficacy of fluorescent lights

The luminous efficacy of the fluorescent light bulb may exceed above 100 Lumens/watt, which is several times higher than the efficacy of an incandescent bulb with similar light output. The incandescent and fluorescent lamps consist of filaments in glass bulbs, whereas LEDs contain small capsules/lenses where tiny chips are placed on a high thermal conductivity material (which acts as the heat sink).

LEDs, typically, just fade gradually. Conventional light bulbs waste most of their energy as heat. For example, an incandescent bulb gives off 90 per cent of its energy as heat; while a compact fluorescent bulb wastes 80 per cent as heat. LEDs remain cool. In addition, because they contain no glass components, they are not vulnerable to vibration or breakage like conventional bulbs.

LED lamps.

Fluorescent light inside a CPU.

Colourful LED lights.

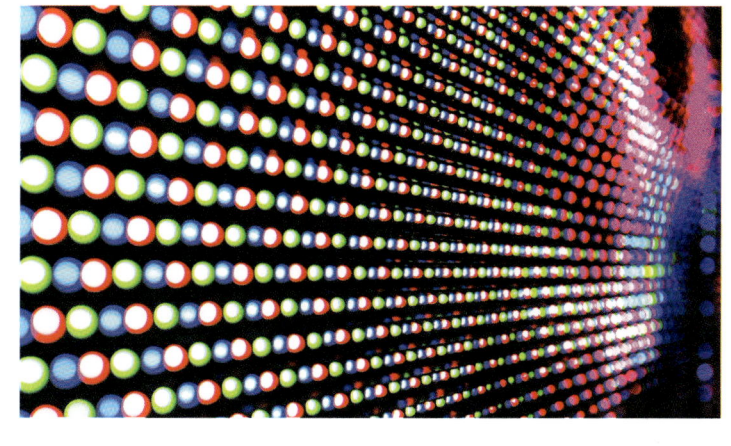

Applications of fluorescent lamps

The compact fluorescent lamp utilises the auxiliary electronics into the base of the lamp, enabling them to fit into a regular light bulb socket. Fluorescent lamps can be used in kitchens, basements or garages. Furthermore, special fluorescent lights are used in stage lighting for film and video production. These lamps are cooler than traditional halogen light sources and use high-frequency ballasts.

SCIENCE ENCYCLOPEDIA

Filament

An incandescent light globe is the most common type of lighting used in our homes. It consists of a very fine and coiled tungsten or sometimes molybdenum filaments that are raised to white heat by passing an electric current through them. The filament is held in position by two support posts that are insulated. They are supported by a glass base. The glass envelope of the globe retains an inert atmosphere around the tungsten filament so that it does not burn.

Working of a bulb

In a light bulb, an electric current is sent through a resistive material. Typically, materials will glow before reaching a melting point and most materials will glow a dull red colour when they reach around 525 °C. Filaments are made from materials that have a high melting point. Tungsten can reach up to 3422 °C before melting. The carbon arc lamp reaches the highest temperature of 3500 °C. Other materials have made good filaments or parts of filaments including tantalum, molybdenum and carbon.

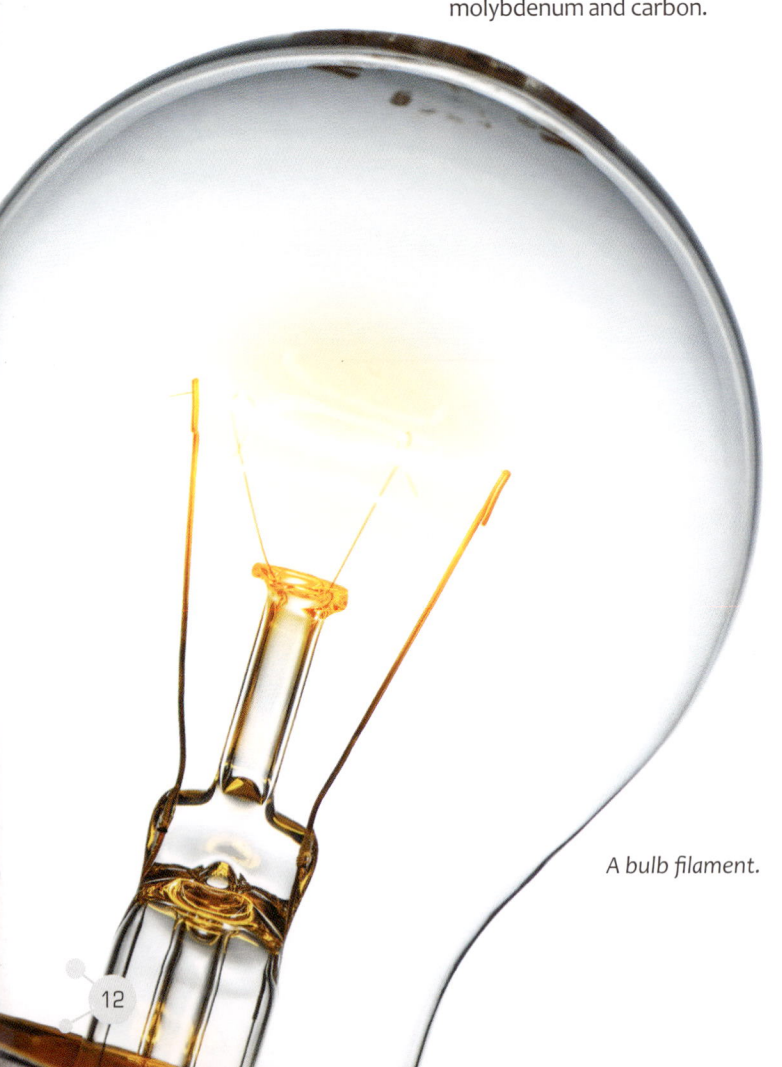

A bulb filament.

History of light filaments

In 1802, Cornish chemist Sir Humphry Davy discovers incandescence in a platinum wire.

In 1841, English inventor Frederick de Moleyns patents an incandescent lamp within a glass bulb and partial vacuum.

In 1879, English physicist Sir Joseph Swan starts working with incandescent light; however, his invention is developed at the same time as Thomas Edison. Swan uses carbonised paper as a filament in a partially evacuated bulb, which lasts several hours.

In 1879, Thomas Edison is able to succeed in creating the first reliable light bulb. His bulbs last almost 600 hours.

In 1902, German chemist Werner von Bolton discovers that using tantalum for a filament increases efficiency, durability and bulb life. The age of metallic filaments begins and Siemens and Halske hold the patent.

In 1904, American chemist Willis Whitney counters the threat from the tantalum lamp with a GEM lamp: a unique process which generates a metallised filament.

In 1904, German chemist Alexander Just and Croatian inventor Franz Hanaman patent a sintered tungsten filament. Tungsten proves to be a good material; however, it is fragile and hard to work with.

In 1912, American chemist Irving Langmuir develops three important improvements to the bulb by developing an argon and nitrogen-filled bulb, tightly coiled filament and a thin molecular hydrogen coating on the inside of the bulb.

Sir Humphry Davy

Thomas Edison

Irving Langmuir

MACHINES

A machine is defined as a system that makes the life of human beings easy. Every machine in this world requires energy to work; this energy can be thermal, mechanical, electrical, light or any other form. The complexity of machines varies with the functions that they are made to perform. Simple machines like the pulley (a wheel rolled around a rope or chain that raises the load), lever (rigid bar on which the load rests), wedge (an object with one sharp end used to cut objects), wheel (the simplest machine that helps to move a load), inclined plane (an inclined surface at any angle used for lifting heavy objects at a height, e.g. ramps) and screw are very less complex as compared to machines, such as the computer, automobile or radio.
These simple machines don't require much force and energy to work. They just require a single human force and they work against this force, which is when we say that work is done.

SCIENCE ENCYCLOPEDIA

Efficiency of Machines

Machines convert input energy into motion. Electrical motors used in household chores require high voltage of power supply to be able to extract underground water. The efficiency of machines is a useful element as it compares the input and output of energy.

What is a machine's efficiency?

A typical machine helps in changing the direction or magnitude of a force using the force that has been provided from a specific input. This input is in the form of energy. The work done by the machine is the creation of a motion against a resistive force. The efficiency of the machine helps in conserving energy as well. If a machine is highly efficient, it will make use of minimum energy to give maximum output. Hence, while judging any machine, its efficiency is used to rate its quality. Therefore, when buying a machine, for example, a refrigerator, we consider the amount of energy it consumes and the amount of cooling it provides. If the cooling is greater than the energy consumption, then the machine is efficient.

Light weight machine parts are used for efficient running of the aircraft.

Increasing efficiency

Engineers, scientists and designers keep looking for ways to increase the efficiency of engines. Efficiency can be enhanced by many innovative ways. However, the simplest way to do this is by reducing the weight of the machine. This can be achieved by choosing lightweight material for its construction. Therefore, the strength to weight ratio of any material is an extremely important parameter. Operating the machine at a higher temperature is another way to increase efficiency. Similarly, choosing other design parameters can improve efficiency. But the fact is that conceptualising or incorporating changes to enhance efficiency is not an easy task.

FUN FACT

The efficiencies of different machines are different. The amount of energy that you use to heat water using an electric geyser for one bath is enough to keep the bulb in your house lighted for 3 months!

Barometer

A barometer is an instrument employed to measure atmospheric pressure, also known as air pressure or barometric pressure and the weight of air.

Invention

In 1643, Italian physicist and mathematician Evangelista Torricelli invented the barometer. He started by inverting a simple glass test tube (4 feet in length) filled with mercury into a dish. He realised that the mercury did not flow out of the tube, but a small amount of vacuum was created in the tube. He further observed that the amount of vacuum created varied from time to time and place to place. He was able to relate this change in vacuum to the atmospheric pressure at the given point of time. The Fortin Barometer is an improved version of the barometer. It has been proven that this advanced version of the barometer gives a clearer result than any other.

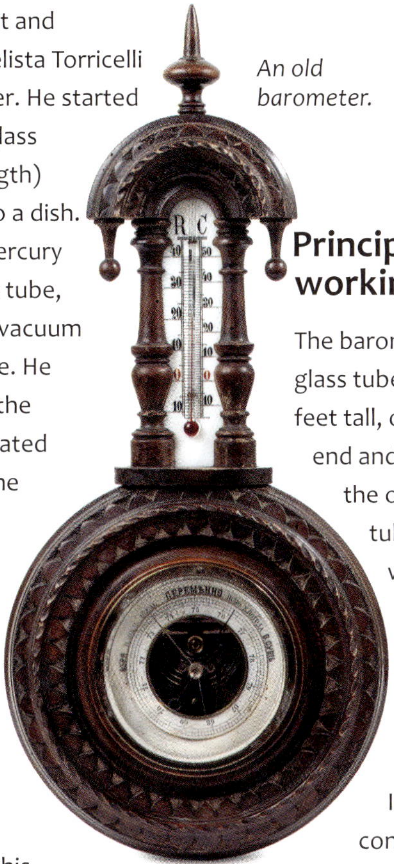

An old barometer.

Principle of working

The barometer is a glass tube that is 3 feet tall, open at one end and sealed at the other. This tube is filled with mercury and placed inverted in a container known as a reservoir. It basically contains mercury that falls into the tube and creates a vacuum at the top. To properly operate the barometer, it is given a balanced weight. If the weight of mercury is less than the level of air pressure, the mercury level rises in the tube and vice versa. Thus, to check the proper measurement, it is important to keep the mercury and vacuum weight balanced.

An old glass barometer showing air pressure with the help of dials.

Applications

Aneroid Barometer is a type of barometer that does not make use of any liquid. Thus, this kit is mainly used as an altimeter in aircrafts. A low pressure or sudden fall of pressure indicates uncommon weather, whereas a high pressure indicates fine weather.

The change in atmosphere pushes the top of the metal box upwards or downwards. This is rigged into a circular dial with a hand that magnifies the movement of the box and points to a number around the circumference of the dial.

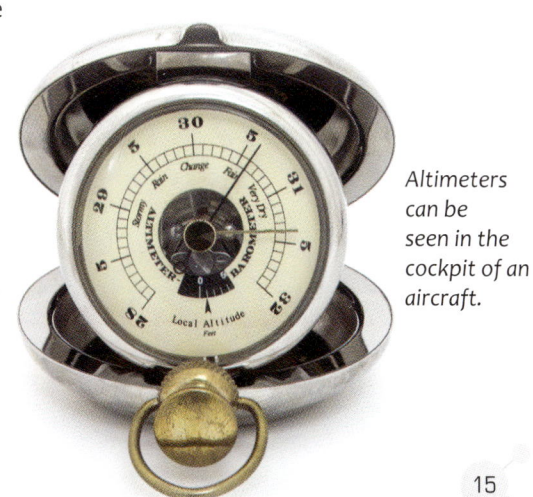

Altimeters can be seen in the cockpit of an aircraft.

SCIENCE ENCYCLOPEDIA

Induction Heater

Induction heating is a process that bonds, hardens or softens metals or other conductive materials. Induction heating offers an attractive combination of speed, consistency and control.

Invention

In 1831, Michael Faraday discovered the principle of induction heating. When an alternating electrical current is applied to the primary of a transformer, an alternating magnetic field is generated. According to Faraday's law, if the secondary of a transformer is located within the magnetic field, then an electric current would be induced.

Initially, this discovery was simply used to avoid the overheating of motors and transformers. However, by the twentieth century, the need arose to find more efficient ways of generating heat, mainly in order to melt industrial steel. This is when the laws of Faraday were brought into use and induction heating took main stage. Today, we use induction heating in our daily household appliances as well.

Passing a current through the metal coil causes the formation of a magnetic field, which, in turn, generates heat.

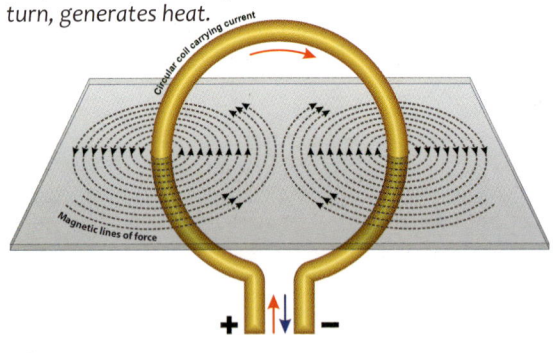

Principle of working

Induction heating relies on the unique characteristics of radio frequency (RF) energy, which is a part of the electromagnetic spectrum below infrared and microwave energy. As heat gets transferred to the object through electromagnetic waves, the object never witnesses direct contact with any flame. Also, the inductor does not get hot and there is no product contamination. If the process parameters are standardised, the process can be replicated and controlled. In basic induction heating, a solid state RF power supply transmits an AC current through an inductor (often a copper coil) and the part to be heated (the work piece) is placed inside the inductor. The heating usually occurs with both magnetic and non-magnetic parts, and is often denoted as the "Joule effect".

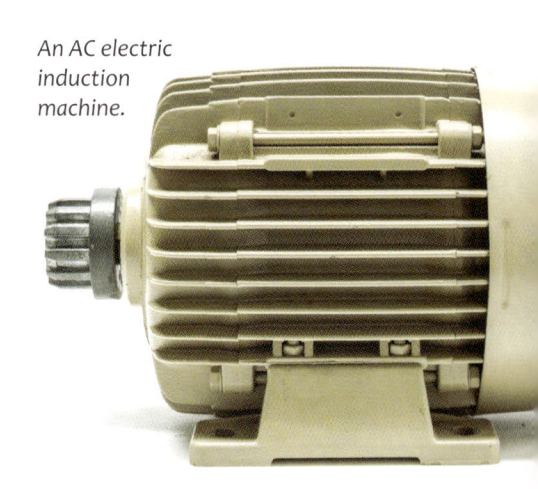

An AC electric induction machine.

Applications

One of the major applications of induction heating is in vacuum furnaces. Induction cookers are widely used for cooking purposes. Sometimes, induction heating is also used to expand an item to fit it at a specific spot. Presently, induction welding, brazing and furnaces are also used.

Induction heating furnace used for heating steel.

LIGHT, MACHINES AND PARTICLE PHYSICS

Generator

It is difficult to imagine our life without electricity. What happens when there is a power failure? We use a generator. The generator is a device that converts mechanical energy into electrical energy.

Industrial power generator.

Invention

In 1831, English chemist and physicist Michael Faraday and American physicist Joseph Henry almost simultaneously discovered the principle of operation of generators.

Principle of working

There is a basic principle on which different types of generators work, but the details of construction may differ. A coil of wire is placed within a magnetic field, with its ends attached to an electrical device, such as a galvanometer. When the coils are rotated within the magnetic field, the galvanometer displays a current being induced within the coil. Generators can be sub-divided into two major categories depending on whether the electric current generated is alternating current (AC) or direct current (DC). An AC generator can be modified to produce DC electricity as well. The change requires a commutator, which is a slip ring. The brushes are attached to both halves of the commutators. They are placed in such a way that the brushes slip from one half to the other the moment the direction of the current in the coil is reversed.

Applications

In an electrical generator, the galvanometer is substituted by an electrical device. Electrical generators are used to power many electrical systems, like those within a car. One of the major practical applications of generators is in the production of prominent amounts of electrical energy for industrial and residential use.

Electronic galvanometer.

17

SCIENCE ENCYCLOPEDIA

Furnace

The furnace is used as a heating element at a very high temperature. It is built to produce useful heat by combustion or other means. Coal furnaces, gas-fired furnaces and electrical furnaces are widely used in many industries.

Invention

The German-born British inventor Sir William Siemens first demonstrated the arc furnace in 1879 at the Paris Exposition by melting iron in crucibles. In 1906, the first commercial arc furnace was installed in the USA; it had a capacity of four tonnes and was equipped with two electrodes.

Melting Iron.

A furnace that uses coal as fuel.

Principle of working

Furnaces can be distinguished based on their uses. The basic principle of a furnace is that chemical energy is converted into heat by burning fuels, such as coal, wood, oil and hydrocarbon gases. In an electric furnace or burner, electrical energy is converted into heat.

Electric burner.

Applications

Electric furnaces produce roughly two-fifths of the steel made in the USA. They are used by speciality steelmakers to produce almost all the stainless steel, aluminium alloy, cast alloy and special alloys, which are required by chemical, automotive, aircraft, food processing and other industries. Electric furnaces are also employed exclusively by mini-mills and small plants that use scrap charges to produce reinforcing and merchant bars.

FUN FACT
The Romans were the earliest humans to use a furnace around 1200 BCE. They called it "hypocausts". They used it to heat their houses, quite like the central heating systems that we use today.

Hot steel in a furnace.

LIGHT, MACHINES AND PARTICLE PHYSICS

Periscope

It would be exciting to travel underwater by a submarine. However, how do the seamen know what is happening over the sea level? The answer is very simple. They make use of a periscope. A periscope helps one to see objects above or below their eye level.

Invention

The first periscope was marketed in the 1430s by German goldsmith Johannes Gutenberg. Furthermore, it was only in 1647 that a periscope with lenses was made by the famous astronomer Johannes Hevelius.

Principle of working

The periscope is an optical instrument, a device consisting of two mirrors or reflecting prisms set parallel to each other at an angle of 45 degrees. These two mirrors help in changing the direction of light coming from the scene observed. The first mirror deflects it down through a vertical tube while the second mirror diverts it horizontally to allow convenient viewing. If the two mirrors are placed at 90 degrees, it helps to see the view behind the viewer.

Applications

Periscopes of this type were widely used during World War II in tanks and other armoured vehicles as observation devices. When fitted with a small, auxiliary gun-sight telescope, the tank periscope can also be used for pointing and firing guns. Defence personnel also use a periscope in gun turrets. The periscope is used in naval wars when, sometimes, there is low visibility. It also enables an observer to see his/her surroundings while remaining undercover, behind the armour or submerged. In addition, periscopes are also used to see into nuclear reactors.

Soldiers using a periscope behind their bunker to scout for enemies.

SCIENCE ENCYCLOPEDIA

Steam Engine

Every machine requires energy to work. The steam engine is a type of machine that requires steam to work. In this machine, heat energy is converted into mechanical energy.

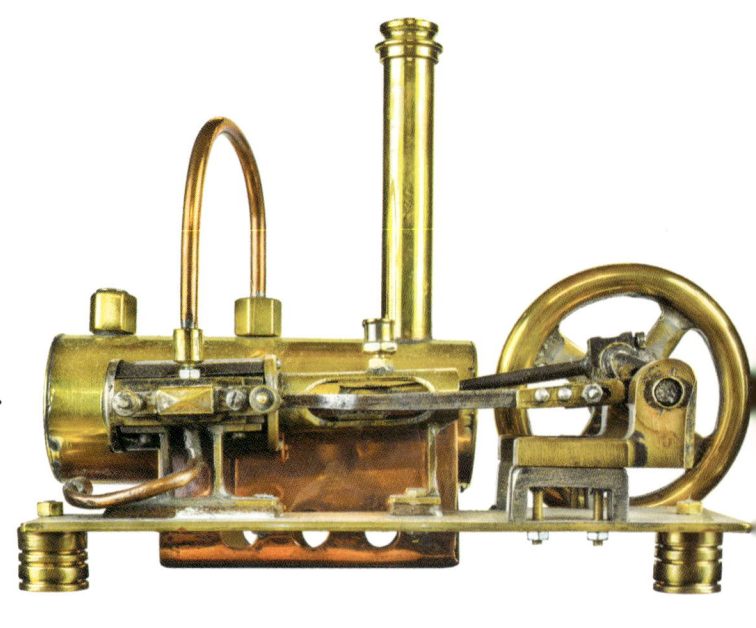

Old style steam machine.

Furnace in steam train.

Invention

The steam engine was first brought into existence in the first century by Hero of Alexandria, but it was not used commercially back then. In 1698, English engineer Thomas Savery invented the steam engine that could pump water. In 1712, English inventor Thomas Newcomen developed the steam engine with a piston. In 1781, Scottish mechanical engineer James Watt gave us the first steam engine that worked with continuous rotary motion. Separate condensing techniques were used to avoid the heating of the cylinder in each cycle. They slowly became a primary source for the production of power and electricity. Initially, steam engines were used in rotary machines, power looms, automobile industries, mills and agriculture. With advancements in science and technology, the steam engine was improvised and steam turbines started being used for the generation of electricity. Commercially speaking, the first steam engines were used only to pump water.

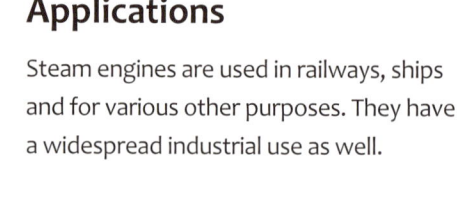

Principle of working

Steam engines supply steam using boilers that expand in the presence of pressure and transform heat into work. The remnant heat energy is allowed to escape. The steam engine has maximum efficiency when the steam is condensed. The condenser temperature should be very low and the pressure should be high. To raise the temperature of steam, it is passed through the super heater; which has a few parallel pipes containing hot gases.

Applications

Steam engines are used in railways, ships and for various other purposes. They have a widespread industrial use as well.

LIGHT, MACHINES AND PARTICLE PHYSICS

Microwave Oven

The microwave oven has become a household device because of its many advantages over conventional ovens. It uses microwaves to create heat within the item that is kept inside it. Depending upon the amount of food, you can adjust the amount of time that you want to heat it for.

Invention

The first microwave oven was unexpectedly discovered by Percy Spencer during World War II as a byproduct of radar research using magnetrons.

Principle of working

Microwave ovens are devices that are used to cook or heat food by using microwaves for their operation. This appliance cooks food by means of high-frequency electromagnetic waves, that is, microwaves, instead of any sort of flame or heat. A microwave oven is a relatively small, box-like oven containing magnetron. Magnetron is responsible for the generation of microwaves, which interact with food particles, primarily water molecules, and increase the temperature of the food. Like all electromagnetic waves, microwaves too have dual polarity and they change their polarity with respect to each cycle, every second. Food particles contain many water molecules, as well as positive and negative poles, which interact with the poles of the microwave. This interaction of the food particles and microwave particles results in the excitation of food particles. The food particles then rotate at double the speed, producing heat, which increases the temperature of the food and cooks it. Microwave particles don't interact with plastic or glass; thus, the container doesn't get affected. This is why it is always advised to use special microwave-oven utensils.

Applications

Microwaves are a form of radiation that occupy a part of the electromagnetic spectrum. Microwaves are called millimetre waves due to their small wavelength. These waves are mostly used in a microwave oven or for satellite communication, medical purposes, etc.

Food can be heated and cooked in a microwave oven.

FUN FACT

Microwave ovens were not always so compact. The first one ever made was the size of a refrigerator, about 6 feet tall. Not only that, it weighed about 350 kg!

SCIENCE ENCYCLOPEDIA

Submarine

Submarines are machines that remain underwater. In 1578, William Bourne, a British mathematician and writer on naval topics, suggested an entirely closed boat that could remain submerged in water, as well as float on water.

Invention

Since the seventeenth century, there has been continuous progress on submarines. Submarines first became a major factor in naval warfare during World War I (1914–18) in both the Atlantic and Pacific, when Germany used surface merchant vessels. They made use of torpedoes, which are underwater missiles. Later, in the 1960s, submarines that remained under water for months or years became the sole weapon during wars. These submarines were nuclear-powered. Thus, submarines loaded with many torpedoes and nuclear missiles were used in the naval wars. Famed American inventor and artist Robert Fulton experimented with submarines for several years before his steamboat Clermont steamed across the Hudson River.

Principle of working

The submarine is a vessel that must be able to float on water, as well as completely submerge underwater. In order for a heavy vessel made of iron to float on water, it is built in a special way. The body of the submarine is made of two layers. There is an inner layer and an outer layer. The space between the inner and outer layer is the air chamber. If the submarine is floating and has to submerge, then pumps fitted on the outer layer pull in water and fill the air chamber with water, causing the submarine to sink. When the submarine has to float again, pressurised air is pushed into the air chamber, causing the submarine to come to the surface and float again.

Applications

A submarine, unlike any naval vessel, is capable of propelling itself beneath the water, as well as on the water's surface. It cannot be compared to the normal surface ships. This property of submarines makes them capable enough to be used in wars. Submarines are used to extract oil from deep sea. They are also used in the tourism sector and for exploring underwater living environments.

The crew of a submarine.

A submarine appearing at sea-level.

LIGHT, MACHINES AND PARTICLE PHYSICS

Telescopes

A telescope is a typically long tube of metal with a lens at each end that helps us to see faraway objects. Telescopes are used to examine celestial bodies like the moon, Earth and stars. They are also used by sailors to search far-off horizons for the sight of land.

Invention

In the seventeenth century, Galileo was the first person to include a telescope in the study of celestial bodies called astronomy. Prior to this, no magnification instruments were used. With new progress in science and technology, more powerful telescopes have been developed that can magnify any small part of space. In addition to advancement in telescopes, there are more optical instruments like cameras, microscopes and spectrographs. Such developments have contributed a lot to the exploration of space and knowing things that would be impossible to know without their existence.

Principle of working

When light travels from one medium to another, it bends either towards or away from the focal point of the medium. This process is called refraction. Light changes path only when the densities of two mediums are different. Similarly, a telescope uses the process of refraction. There is a two-lens arrangement in a telescope: objective lens and eyepiece lens. The outer one is the objective lens from which light enters the telescope. The eyepiece lens enlarges the image of the object being viewed. The second lens is the eyepiece lens, which enlarges the image of the object.

A coin viewer.

Applications

The telescope is used to capture magnified images of bodies in space and even on Earth. It helps in space exploration. Telescope plays a key role in astronomy. They help to study the nature of various celestial bodies like comets, meteors, planets, Milky Way and other galaxies.

SCIENCE ENCYCLOPEDIA

Thermometer

The thermometer is very common device used in our daily lives. Over the years, its general principle was improved after experiments were carried on with liquids like mercury. A scale was also provided to measure the expansion and contraction caused by these liquids with a rise and fall in temperature.

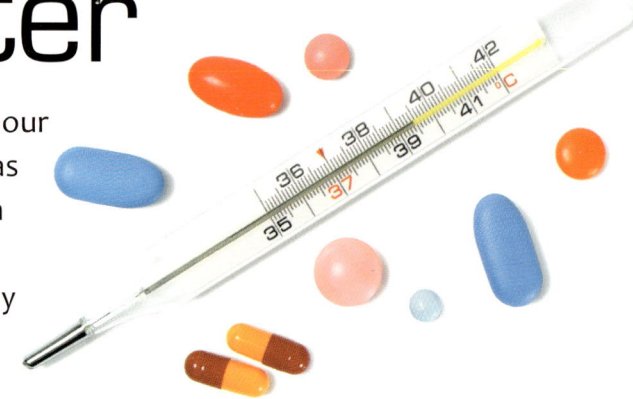

Invention

Famous Italian mathematician–physicist Galileo Galilei invented the thermometer.

Substances sensitive to changes in temperature, like mercury, are utilised in a thermometer. Different types of thermometers are available, such as gas and liquid thermometers. Gas thermometers generally work at very low temperatures. The commonly used ones are liquid thermometers that usually have mercury enclosed in a sealed glass tube with nitrogen gas around it. Mercury thermometers are simple to use, inexpensive and can be used to measure a wide temperature span.

Galileo thermometer.

FUN FACT

Thermometer is an improved product. Before it, there was a thermoscope that only indicated if the object was getting hotter or colder!

Applications

The thermometer is used mostly in industries, research and laboratories. They are used wherever we need to measure temperature.

Electrical resistance thermometer.

Principle of working

There are several types of thermometers. Electrical-resistance thermometers use platinum and operate on the principle that electrical resistance varies with changes in temperature. Thermocouples are composed of two wires made of different materials joined together at one end and exposed to temperature. The other end is attached to a voltage measuring device. When there is a temperature difference, a voltage is generated between the two ends. Magnetic thermometers work best at low temperatures. As the temperature decreases, their efficiency increases, due to which they are believed to measure low temperatures with more accuracy.

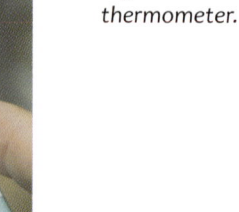

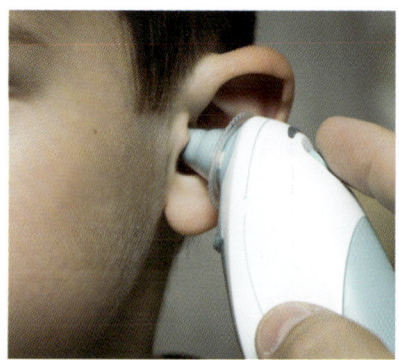

Digital thermometer.

Clinical thermometer.

24

LIGHT, MACHINES AND PARTICLE PHYSICS

Turbines

Turbines are machines that convert the energy in a stream of flowing body into work by passing the flowing body through the blades of a rotor. When higher velocity flowing bodies exert force on the rotor, the blades move and work is performed. Turbines can be classified according to the flowing bodies used: water, steam, gas and wind.

Steam turbine.

Invention

In 1888, American engineer Lester Allen Pelton designed the first modern turbine, which was more efficient, to produce mechanical energy. When the free water stream strikes the turbine buckets tangentially, the flow of the stream gets equally divided in both directions.

Applications

Wind turbines are modified variations of windmills that have been a major source of electricity in many parts of the world, including the USA. Presently, the primary use of water turbines is for electric power generation.

Principle of working

Steam turbines are efficient machines as they produce the maximum amount of electrical energy. A steam turbine is driven by the steam produced by either fossil fuels or nuclear power. The output energy extracted from the steam is expressed according to change of temperature across the turbine. The change of temperature by steam increases with the pressure of the steam generator and with reduced turbine-exit pressure. In gas turbines, the flowing body is a mixture of air and other gaseous products of combustion. Gas-turbine engines consist of a compressor, turbine and many other complex parts. A water turbine uses the potential energy of water to provide mechanical energy.

Gas turbine.

The turbines of an aircraft.

SCIENCE ENCYCLOPEDIA

Electric Motor

A machine that converts mechanical energy to electrical energy is called an electric generator. On the other hand, an electrical machine that converts electrical energy into mechanical energy is called an electric motor. Electric motors are a part of every electrical appliance, that we find around us, whose output is mechanical energy in some form.

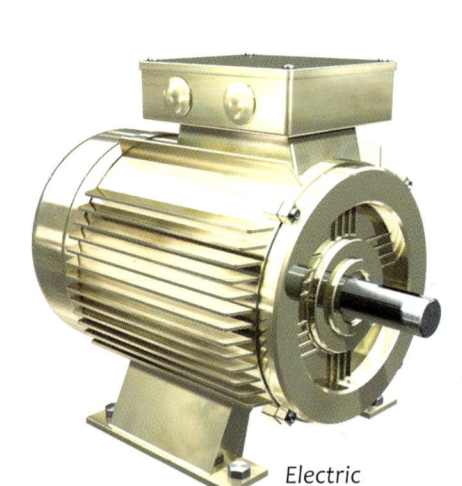

Invention

In the 1740s, the first ever electric motor, a simple electrostatic device, was invented by a Scottish monk, Andrew Gordon. In 1827, Hungarian physicist Ányos Jedlik invented the electromagnetic self-rotors that delivered relatively weak electric currents. In May 1834, the first actual electric motor that could deliver a significant amount of mechanical output power was invented by Prussian engineer and physicist Moritz von Jacobi. The present day electric motor was invented in 1886 by American inventor Frank Julian Sprague and can produce a considerable amount of power under various amounts of electrical loads.

Electric motor.

Principle of working

An electric motor generally runs on the principle of Fleming's Left Hand Rule. An armature is placed between two magnetic poles. When an electric current is passed through the armature, they create a rotating magnetic field. This rotating magnetic field takes hold of the rotor and makes it spin around. Any form of machine that runs on an electric motor is then physically built around this rotating rotor.

For example, let's take a look at a toy car. When you put batteries in the car, an electric current gets passed through the rotor in the electric motor of the car. This will create rotating magnetic energy, causing the rotor to rotate. When the rotor begins to rotate, a network of wheels connected to the rotor will begin to rotate, which in turn will make the wheels of the toy car rotate. This is how the toy car ends up running on a pair of batteries.

Applications

Electric motors have a wide range of applications. They are used in water pumps, refrigerators, vacuum cleaners, cars, fans and so on.

Electric fan.

Electric car at a charging station.

PARTICLE PHYSICS

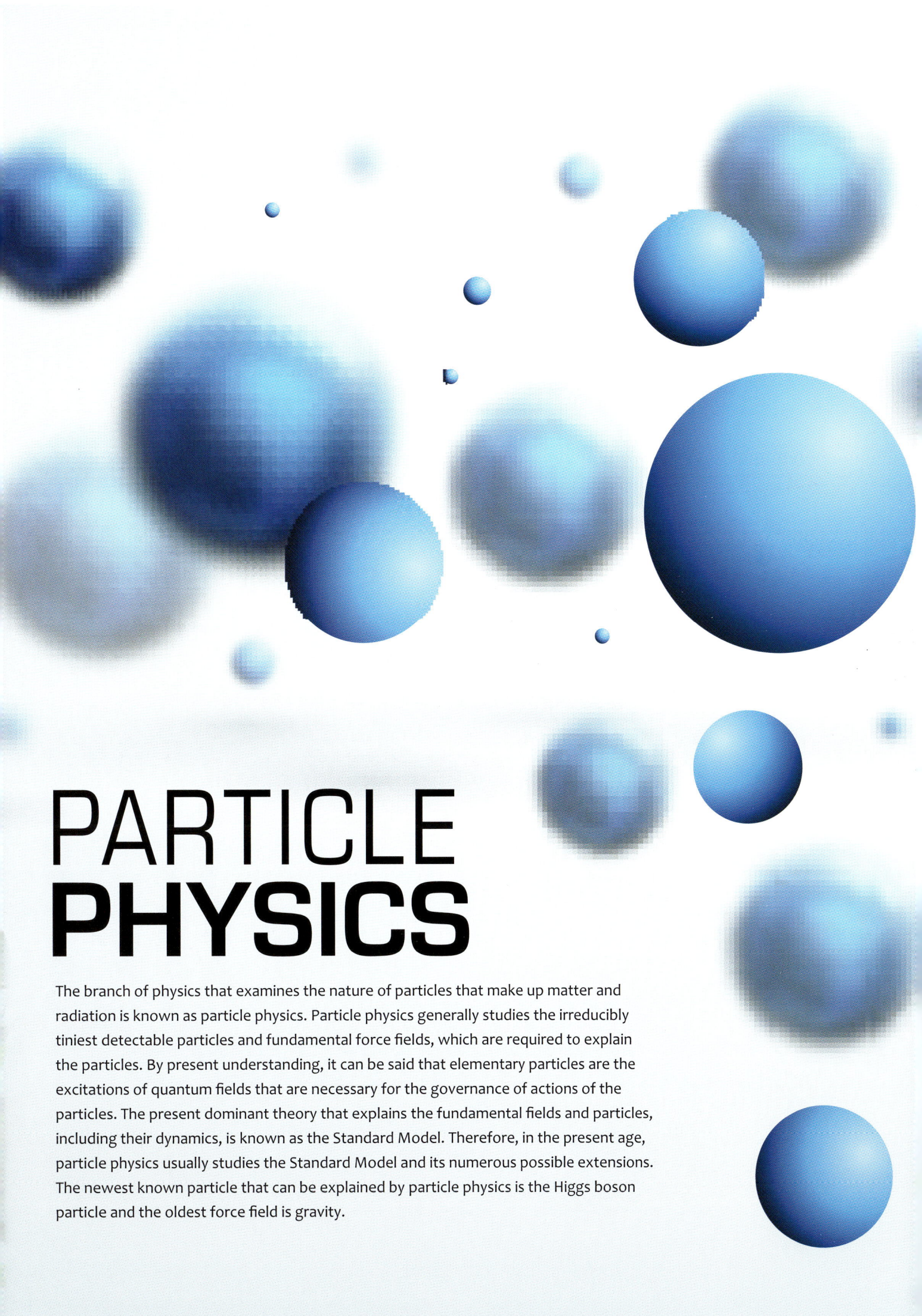

The branch of physics that examines the nature of particles that make up matter and radiation is known as particle physics. Particle physics generally studies the irreducibly tiniest detectable particles and fundamental force fields, which are required to explain the particles. By present understanding, it can be said that elementary particles are the excitations of quantum fields that are necessary for the governance of actions of the particles. The present dominant theory that explains the fundamental fields and particles, including their dynamics, is known as the Standard Model. Therefore, in the present age, particle physics usually studies the Standard Model and its numerous possible extensions. The newest known particle that can be explained by particle physics is the Higgs boson particle and the oldest force field is gravity.

SCIENCE ENCYCLOPEDIA

Splitting an Atom

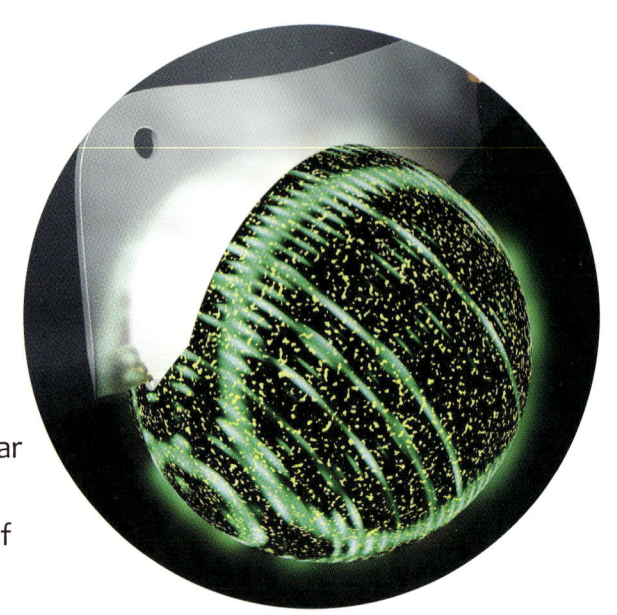

Splitting an atom is also termed as a fission reaction. Nuclear fission reaction is basically the splitting of any heavy nucleus, when it absorbs neutrons.
Otto Hahn, in 1938, discovered the phenomena of nuclear fission. Nuclear fission can take place naturally or heavy nucleus can be made fissionable by the bombardment of neutrons, known as induced fission.

History

In 1932, in England, James Chadwick discovered the neutron, which began the discovery of nuclear fission. Then in 1939, German physicists Lise Meitner and Otto Frisch first coined the term fission. It was used to explain the disintegration of a heavy nucleus into two lighter nuclei of almost equal size. Heavy elements, including uranium, thorium and plutonium, can undergo spontaneous fission, a form of radioactive decay, as well as induced fission, a form of artificial nuclear reaction.

A weapon of mass destruction: Nuclear bomb made from uranium.

Co-relation of nuclear fission and energy

The nuclear fission of any heavy nucleus needs an energy input of about 7 million electron volts (MeV). This is the amount of energy required to overcome the attractive nuclear forces, which hold the core, that is, the nucleus, in its shape.

The isotopes, which undergo induced fission after being struck by the free neutron are known as fissionable. They can be used as nuclear fuel to produce energy; for example, 233U, 235U and 239Pu.

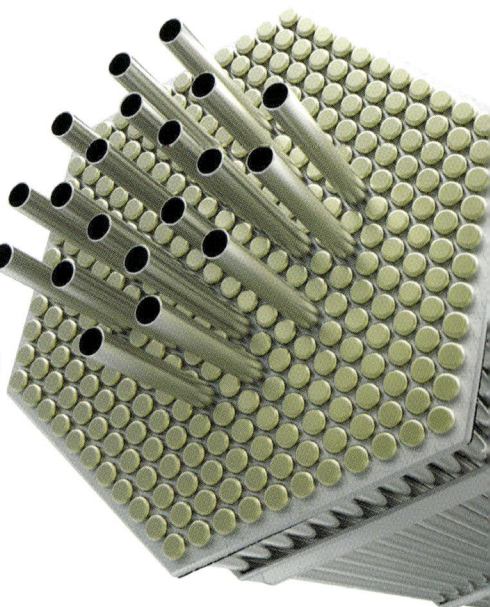

The produced neutrons sustain a chain reaction because each atom that splits, releases excess neutrons, which cause the neighbouring atoms to split. The aftermath of the splits is the release of enormous amount of energy in the form of heat. This heat is utilised to heat up the coolant that goes off to the turbine and generator to produce electricity.

Nuclear fuel assembly.

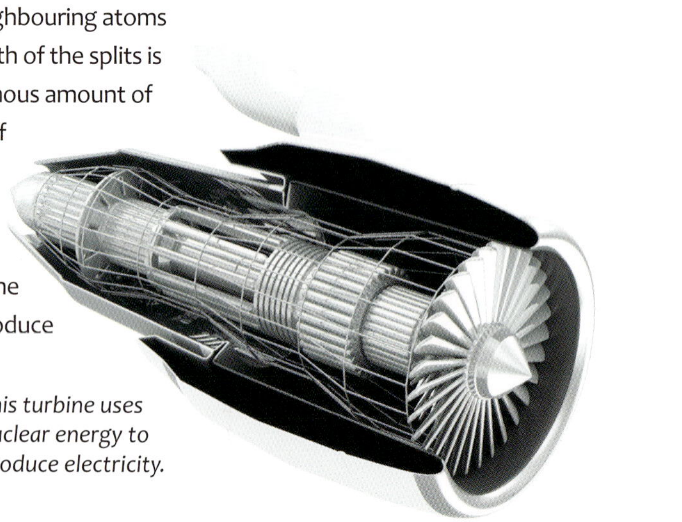

This turbine uses nuclear energy to produce electricity.

LIGHT, MACHINES AND PARTICLE PHYSICS

Fatal Fusion

Nuclear fusion is the method by which two atoms, belonging to elements with lower atomic number, are made to react with one another to form a heavier atom, releasing a lot of energy in the process. The amount of energy released by nuclear fusion is much higher than fission and produces fewer by-products.

History

Nuclear fusion is a very exciting field of physics that has captured the interest of scientists all over the world. However, it came into existence almost as soon as the atom was discovered. But its research and studies picked momentum at the end of World War II, when the arms race began. Nuclear fusion came to be used for battle purposes and nuclear bombs, such as Hydrogen Atomic bomb, were invented. Around the late 1940s and 1950s, the scientists got a better understanding of the process. Soon, nuclear fusion was being explored to create clean, renewable energy.

Renewable energy.

FUN FACT
Helium was discovered in the Sun as a by-product of all the nuclear fusion and was named so after the Greek Sun God, Helios.

Types of fusions

There are two types of fusion: one, where two hydrogen atoms combine and two, where one atom of deuterium and one atom of tritium combine. In 1930, German physicist Hans Bethe stated that by fusing two hydrogen atoms, energy can be released that could be harnessed and used for our benefit. However, to be able to do this practically, it would be better to use deuterium and tritium atoms as the rate of the reaction is much higher and the amount of energy released is 40 times that of hydrogen fusion.

Atom bomb used in the war.

Naturally occurring nuclear fusions

The Sun, which is the source of energy for our entire planet, is a hot ball of fire. We know this. However, how does this fire keep burning? How does it not run out of fuel? The answer is simple. The Sun is covered with nuclear fusions that have been going on since millions of years. Without any control, the reaction keeps going on, creating this hot mass of fire that is capable of running an entire solar system.

29

SCIENCE ENCYCLOPEDIA

Nuclear Power

Imagine travelling with a bolt of electricity back through the wall socket, through miles of power lines into the nuclear reactor that generated it. We would find the generator that produces the spark. We would also discover the jet of steam that turns the turbine and finally, the radioactive uranium bundle that turns water into steam.

Nuclear power plants

Nuclear power plants are essentially thermal power plants, where the source of heat energy is the nuclear reaction. In a typical thermal power plant, we have coal with high calorific value as the fuel. We burn this coal to generate heat. This heat in turn converts water into pressurised steam and that does the mechanical work of turning the turbine. That way, heat is converted into mechanical energy. Then, we have the turbine's mechanical energy converted into electricity via the generator. Nuclear power plants employ exactly the same working principle. However, instead of burning coal, we have nuclear rods inside a nuclear reactor.

Control room of a nuclear power station.

Nuclear reaction

The nuclear reactor is where a nuclear chain reaction occurs in a controlled manner. Usually, uranium rods are used in the nuclear fission. A kilogram of uranium can generate three million times more energy than what we get by burning a kilogram of coal. When the nuclei collide with nearby atoms in the nuclear reactor, we have thermal energy. This is used to raise steam. Then, the process proceeds as it would have done in case of any typical thermal power plant.

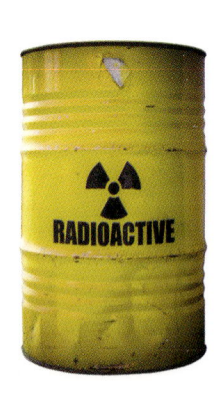

Distribution of nuclear power in the world.

Disadvantages of a nuclear power plant

Nuclear power plants also cause pollution and the waste is radioactive in nature. This means that the waste takes a very long time – hundreds of years – to lose its radioactivity. Discarding nuclear waste is a very difficult task. Again, accidents at nuclear power stations can be fatal. Chernobyl in Russia is a prime example of how bad accidents in nuclear power stations can be.

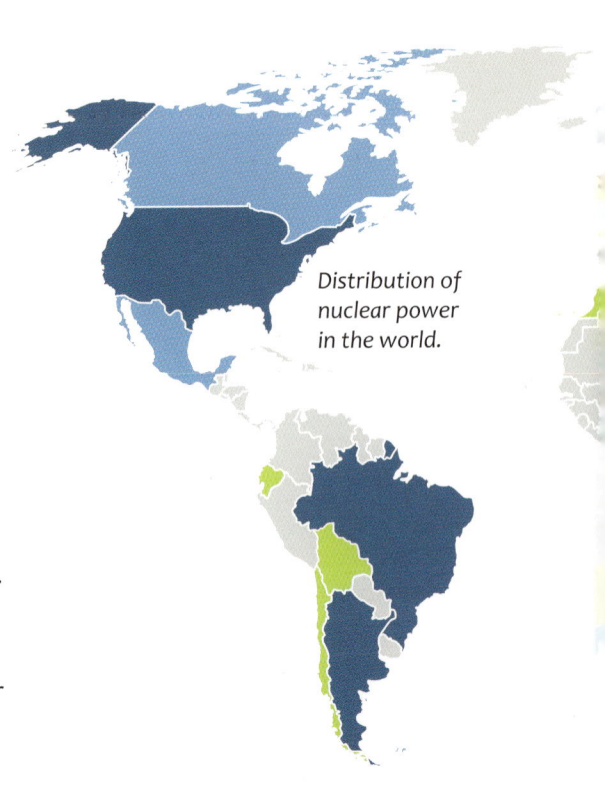

LIGHT, MACHINES AND PARTICLE PHYSICS

What is a nuclear reactor?

Have you thought of what will happen when all the coal in the world exhausts and all the thermal power plants are forced to shut down? How will electricity be generated? To answer that, there are a few solutions that can be an alternative, such as hydro, nuclear and solar energy. Among them, the most prominent one is nuclear energy.

A nuclear power plant uses nuclear reactors for generating electricity. A nuclear reactor is also used to move spacecraft and submarines, produce isotopes for medical and diagnostic uses, and also for conducting research. A nuclear reactor is a mechanical system where sustained and controlled nuclear chain reaction is allowed to take place.

Principle of working

Fuel kept in the reactor vessel takes part in a chain reaction and yields enormous heat. This heat is extracted to produce electricity. Nuclear chain reactions are of two types through which electricity can be generated: (a) fission chain reaction and (b) fusion chain reaction. Utilisation of the released energy during either fission or fusion chain reaction is the main objective in the nuclear power generation methodology.

A nuclear reactor is a part of a nuclear power plant.

FUN FACT

As of 1st March, 2011, there were 443 operating nuclear power reactors across the world in 47 different countries.

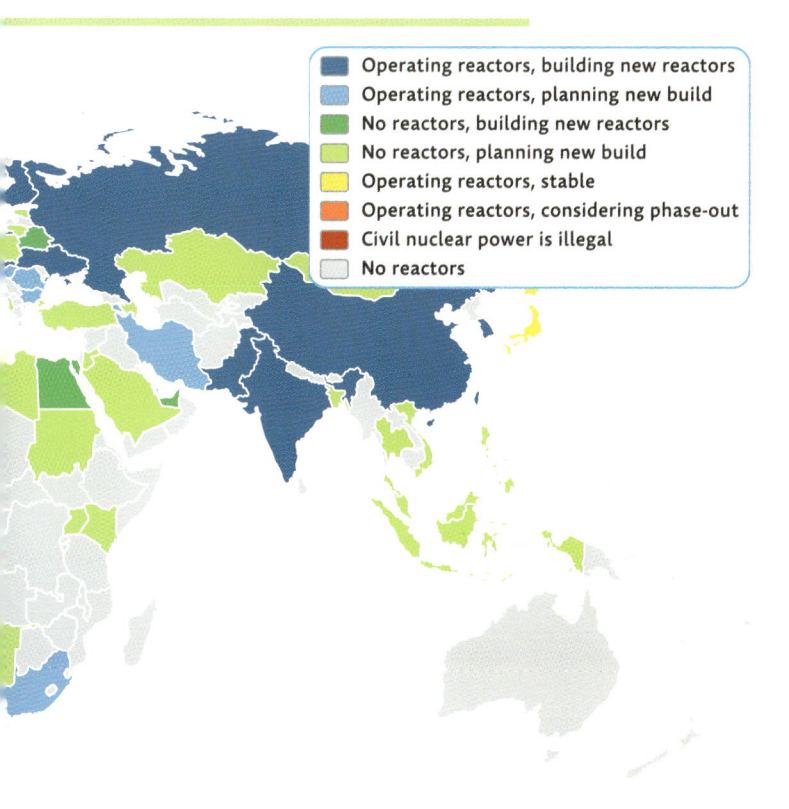

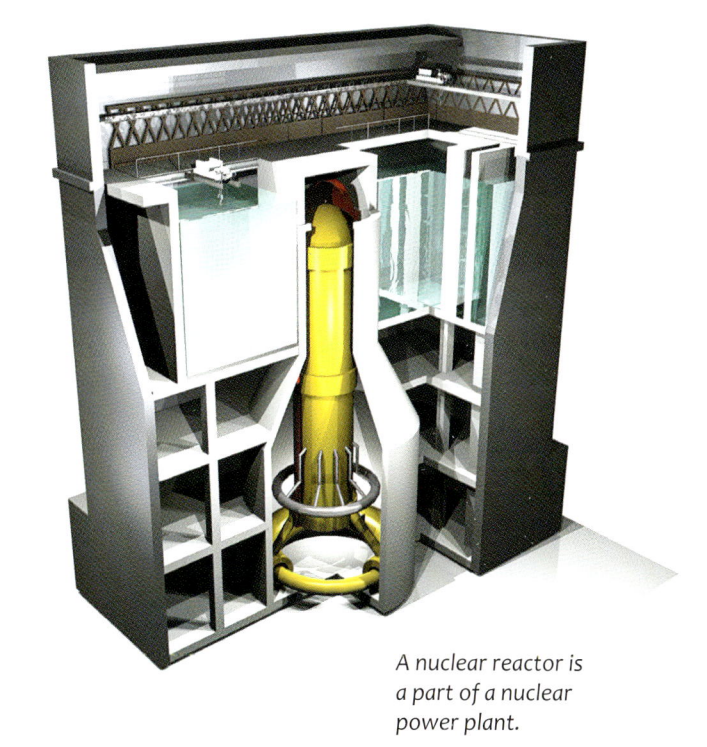

- Operating reactors, building new reactors
- Operating reactors, planning new build
- No reactors, building new reactors
- No reactors, planning new build
- Operating reactors, stable
- Operating reactors, considering phase-out
- Civil nuclear power is illegal
- No reactors

Main components of a nuclear reactor

- **Core** – The core of the reactor contains the nuclear fuel, basically uranium, in the form of bundles.

- **Coolant** – The heat produced during the nuclear reaction is taken out by the coolant. The most common type of coolant is plain water (H_2O), heavy water (D_2O), liquid sodium and helium.

- **Control rods** – These are required for controlling the reaction and shutting down the plant.

- **Turbine** – It transforms the heat taken out by the coolant into electricity like in any other conventional power plant.

- **Containment** – This is the structure that separates the nuclear reactor from the outer environment. These are made of high density, steel reinforced concrete to conceal the harmful radiation inside.

- **Cooling towers** – These require some time to dump the excess heat, which cannot be converted into electricity because of the limitation imposed by the laws of thermodynamics.

Cooler tower on a nuclear power plant.

SCIENCE ENCYCLOPEDIA

Quantum Physics

Quantum physics is a branch of physics, where we deal with the interactions going on inside an atom. At an atomic level, we study about subatomic particles and radiations. The word quantum means energy or unit. It is the smallest amount of energy, which can act on its own.

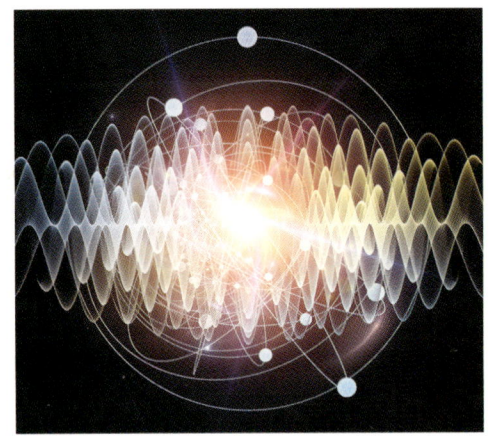

An atom with quantum waves.

Birth of quantum physics

Quantum physics originated in the 1920s to study and describe the laws of physics that are applicable to tiny objects. There were certain facts that classic physics was unable to answer and so, many theories were invented, like photoelectric effect, black-body radiation, atomic theory, corpuscular theory of light and Heisenberg's principle of uncertainty.

Principles of quantum physics

1. Quantum mechanics successfully explained the wave particle or the dual nature of matter.
2. It explained that we cannot simultaneously determine the position and momentum of a particle to high precision.
3. It also explained the basis of quanta, which is the smallest packet of energy.

FUN FACT

The nucleus of an atom is quite small. If you magnify an atom to the size of a football field, the nucleus will only be the size of a marble.

Scientists who contributed

Max Planck is known as the father of quantum theory. Many scientists were involved in the foundation of quantum mechanics. Niels Bohr, Werner Heisenberg, Louis de Broglie, Arthur Compton, Albert Einstein, Erwin Schrodinger, Max Born, John von Neumann and several other scientists made important contributions in this field.

Applications

Traditionally, quantum mechanics works in a subatomic world, but it can clearly explain the working of superconductors, super fluids and many other large organic molecules. Many modern technologies are based on this branch of physics; for example, laser, electron microscope, magnetic resonance imaging, etc.

Cutting a metal sheet using a laser beam works on quantum mechanics.

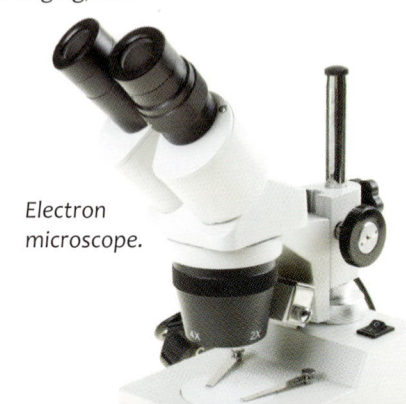

Electron microscope.